pressure cooker love bomb

create love

pressure cooker love bomb

Sharanpal Ruprai

Frontenac House Poetry

Book design: Neil Petrunia, Epix Design
Cover Image: age fotostock / Alamy Stock Photo
Author photo: David Kenney

Library and Archives Canada Cataloguing in Publication

Title: Pressure cooker love bomb / Sharanpal Ruprai.
Names: Ruprai, Sharanpal Kaur, 1977- author.
Description: Poems.
Identifiers: Canadiana 20190062983 | ISBN 9781927823835 (softcover)
Classification: LCC PS8635.U77 P73 2019 | DDC C811/.6—dc23

Frontenac House gratefully acknowledges the support of the Canada Council
for the Arts for our publishing program. We would also like to thank the
Government of Alberta Multimedia Development Fund for their support of our
publishing program.

Canada Council Conseil des Arts
for the Arts   du Canada

Alberta Government

Printed and bound in Canada
Published by Frontenac House Ltd.
37 Westridge Crescent
Okotoks, Alberta T1S 0G7
Tel: 403-263-7025

frontenachouse.com

Second printing January 2022

For Lisha
who learns all her love lines from movies

contents

poems not recipes

poems pressure cooked
marinated set on love

poems instant pot famous
small bites
#lovebombs

how to cook like your punjabi mum
#withoutkillingyourself

to make rotis:

mix 2 cups of atta with 1 cup water.
add a bit of olive oil or ghee to soften the dough.
knead dough until
your upper biceps constrict
your triceps relax
beads of sweat form on your forehead.
stop. repeat.
until dough releases
off your fingers.
let the dough rest.
you, do not rest.

start the daal:
soak dry lentils overnight. in the morning
wash the lentils. drain water, not lentils.
let the water run clear. add water again.
do not worry about wasting water, it comes out of the tap
in abundance. make sure the lentils are covered in water.
add a pinch of salt.
set to boil for fifteen minutes.
do not leave the kitchen.

#dontnapwhilecooking

i rinse yellow lentils and set them to boil. after one hour, the water evaporates. after two the lentils fuse to the to the bottom of the pot. after three, in the middle of my beauty rest, the smoke detector beeps — an alarm clock — the firefighter — said i was lucky to be alive. purchase a timer, a cute one in the shape of a strawberry or apple, hang it around your neck if you plan to nap while cooking.

form dough ball, roughly palm size
slap it back and forth as you would a snowball.

take dough ball between your thumb and index finger
pinch into a flat circle. the flatter the better.

as you are crimping notice how the atta
sprinkles the counter below, this is important.

take up your rolling pin, yes,
the one your mother beat you with.

the rolling pin is your mum's best friend for a reason. think of it as a bat. never argue with anyone in the kitchen. if you are living on your own, a rolling pin makes a good weapon to keep under your bed. just remember it's a rolling pin and it might roll out from under your bed if you stumble and fall hit your head on the hardwood floor give yourself a concussion — the paramedic — will say, you are lucky to be alive. better yet, keep a kirpan under your bed.

roll out dough balls into round even circles.
the thinner the better, make your mum proud.

the trick, keep the dough moving in place.
tenderly enlarging out, light on the rolling pin, slight squeeze.

next, slap the atta-circle on the tava
let it darken, then flip.

no need for a chimta. dough on your fingertips will
form a second skin and protect from burns.

on the jaali, rotis will puff up with steam.
set rotis on a tea-towel. butter one side.

arrange the second roti on top
it will be buttered by the first.

#adultingburns

if you have a chimta, great! pierce a hole in the roti, let the steam out. but remember to quickly turn the deflating roti away from yourself. the steam will scald you. if you're burned, do not, i repeat do not, put butter on the hurt, especially the butter next to the stove. remove the roti off the jaali. nurse your ego with a cold cloth.

add to the lentils: chopped onions, haldi,
garam masala, hari mirch, and salt.
simmer for ten minutes.

set the table with thalis,
homemade rotis, and daal.
now, you can eat.

now, you are
#readyformarriage

#readyformarriage

if you find this all
much too much
then do what punjabi housewives
do;
buy pre-made rotis frozen
vacuum sealed: saag paneer, black daal, kofta with curry
find it in the prepackaged
isle with jars of curry butter chicken sauce.
canadian campers call it magic indian food.

i call it
#readyforlife

nimbu achaar

lemon pickle

always had servants

Chachi observes her mother-in-law's
smooth brown hands, massage a lemon
her palm heavy upon lemon skin
until yellow skin swells slightly
Chachi leans out
Fears lemon juice in the eye.
Chachi does not know how to pickle anything.
The matriarch chef cuts quick
with a dull knife, she refuses to sharpen,
not a drop of juice spews.
And before Chachi can write "cut lemons in fours, after massaging"
in her best British Punjabi English
wedges are squashed into a glass jar
filled with: salt, four whole lal mirch, a thumb of turmeric,
¾ cup of vinegar, sealed with a lid
and chef is ready for her mid-day nap.

passport recipes

Chachi will birth two children,
travel to Chandigarh,
but never back to Nairobi.
She makes nimbu achaar, once
while living in Brampton.
She purchases Patak's pickle
in the condiment isle at Metro;
The recipes will marinate in drawers,
photocopied a few dozen times,
handed to hipster nieces and nephews
when they are ready for marriage
or living on their own.

chili 'n lime

chili peppers from Chacha's backyard
lal-mirchi, hara-mirchi seeds cultivated
over twenty years.

House rule: *don't eat the seeds*, never needed repeating.
chili seeds saved like gold jewelry
for a daughter's bridal dowry.
Seeds wrapped in wax paper, a refinement of heat.
Chacha's gardening hobby
burns our tongues but earns our respect;
learning a trade in a small background garden,
while the rest of us buy red chilis in bulk
at Costco, only to toss
out the jar a year later.

with each passing summer, limes
more expensive at six limes for fifteen dollars.
the only place to find limes
is in Dadiji's backyard in Chandigarh, Sector 21, Punjab.
If you go, do not steal limes,
ask her for one. She will ask,
what you plan to do with them? Do not waste them,
she'll say, limes are difficult to grow.
She'll hand two over, tell you to take another, but do not.
Remember, your lack of food waste habits,
and unseasoned tongue.

upgraded punjab

millennial hipsters insist:
pickling must happen in glass jars
with only organic lemons so to promote a natural ripening
only use whole orange turmeric,
they add ¼ teaspoon of organic dirt to the mix;
their take on living on the land.
from their 20th floor condos
they post mouthwatering Instagram photos

#cantwaittoeat
#readyformarriage

seeking love on sikhnet matrimonial

found poem [updated 2007 and 2018
(poem updated, not website)]

update – marriage assistance

when the gori in the turban
asks about your status
delete your account
ask for your photos to be removed
resist the urge to track down
the happy married couples on the website homepage
and demand your money back
they followed the rules leave them alone
#letlovelive on the internet

#beforemarriage

there is/was seeking love/lust on the internet

browse by:

- women
- women-prefturbanmen
- men
- men turban wearing
- amritdhari men
- amritdhari women
- trans mof
- trans fom
- all of the above

complexion:

- white
- fair
- brown
- wheatish
- dusky
- black
- all the above. tan-up in the summer, lose it in canadian winters

pronouns:

- she/her
- he/him
- they/them
- x

hair:

- i cut my hair
- clean shaven (including down there)
- beard and turban wearing
- turban wearing but clean-shaven beard
- hair everywhere (including down there)
- multicolour – rainbow colours (including down there)

i am a practicing sikh:

- always: wear all five symbols daily
- occasionally:
    - wear four out of the five
    - wear only three on the regular
    - wear two of the five
    - wear only one out of the five daily
- only when food is involved
- never

general cultural values:

- mix of east and west
- eastern
- western
- no values what-so-ever
- depending on the country i am in
- depending on whom i am with
  (and if they are recording videos)

spiritual values:

- highly important to me
- somewhat important to me
- only when food is involved
- not important to me
- i see nanak, jesus, buddha, mohammed, kali, and crows daily

marriage rules one, two, and three
#beforemarriage

a lesson in racism

racism drives on
steady for potholes
do not follow these rules
do not pass them on

read for loopholes
follow the loopholes

marriage rule one

B.M.W.
does not stand for bavarian motor works.
auntyji, tells us to obey and follow.
marriage rules of who we could fall in love with and marry.

> loophole:
> auntyji knows nothing about love or cars.
> auntyji has lived in the uk for too long
> picked up the habit of colonization.

marriage rule two

bbbbbblack.

    disowned from both sides of the family.

mmmmuslim.

    instant disownment.

wwwwwhite.

    might be ok. the children will be light-skinned beige.

    loophole:
    nobody said anything about gender.
    nobody.

marriage rule and three

auntyji instructs us:
fall in love with a
coconut, or a colonizer.
remember life is easier,
if you are both from
the same caste, class, race.

loophole:
nobody said anything about gender.

loophole: nobody
said anything about gender

1. remember aversion

no need for an acronym
or an acrostic poem
to remind us
we don't forget hate
it lives in you, in us,
in our cultural lexicon

2. question everything

when you ask hate about gender
let it be in form of a question:
what is gender?

3. repeat the question

be ready
to laugh with hate
silence with hate
stare back with hate
be ready to repeat
what is gender?
hate is not smart
it does not understand easily
hate is stuck in binaries

4. watch yourself

hate will leave
come back
bubble up like
daal on a stove
but you
know how to deal
with a hate tantrum
turn heat up
pressure up
flip the camera gaze

5. find departures

hate does not
account for ambiguities
find routes
make new escapes

response to marriage rules

#newrules:

love who you love
love who you love
with someone who
you consent with
relax into sexual skin
blur into each other
create new pigments
love who you love that will always be rule one.

do not marry
it's a pressure cooker
try a new language
of forever and together
create a love off
the grid contract
with consent clauses
discussion points
allow for cool off periods
punctuated with added
passion points love off
the grid contracts do not need gender
racism rules or family structure
write a new love contract that will always be rule two.

when someone calls you auntyji
feel the weight of names
hating aunties never
had a chance to be loved
they followed racism rules,
cooking rules, body hair removal rules,
religious rules, a pressure cooker
life of auntyji is not yours
our relationships are new
to you, to them, to us
transform and redefine auntyji that will always be rule three.

bride in a bag

in front of the guru granth sahib
a brown bride barbie
with red n' gold milk-soaked bangles
hung from her stick-like arms
a slight sad smile
a brown bride barbie sat beside
her clean-shaven turban groom
they were a perfect arranged marriage match
she an almost-doctor   he a mechanic
they would have practical children

three years wed
she carries her life in her bride purse at all times
three years later she is living in the basement:
what the almost-doctor does not know —
a mother-in-law will slap her for not cutting the tomatoes
a husband will beat her for not making the bed
her husband has a white girlfriend
her mother-in-law will lock her up
what the almost-doctor does not know —
a rescue
                    is scheduled
bus stop plans for next friday
she will disappear like a snowflake
her parents arrive collect their daughter
thirty-years-old a few years left to search
for a divorcee without children

#leaveforgetmakeanewlife

round-two: a bride-in-a-suitcase
#readyforthenextmarriage

she married a good man
birthed three children
she works in a doctor's lab.
he stays at home with the kids.
she will never come back to canada.
she tells her children stories of backwards sikhs
who live in basements, winnipeg winters
that freeze skin colour white
she becomes an auntyji that match-makes
but only if the families live in the same city.
she is lucky. she an expert on marital relations.

fusion bomb

opt out opt in
create new multi-cooker love
#unsatifactoryinstagrampoetry
#butterchicken/tacoswithroti
#non-binaryaffairs
#youdoyou   seven appliances in one

cardamom and rasgulla

she's the first white girl
i got naked with
campfire between us,
with mugs full of wine, we joke
about coming-of-age stories
with kissing sex scene.
it was hot so we took off all our clothes
ran up a hill at the top we did cartwheels
and somersaults until we flopped in the grass
rolled down the hill

i loved her in blink a of an eye
amber orange danced on her white skin
her large lips stained red between
my thighs over my breasts
in firelight everyone looks tanned

we locked lips all that summer
i showed her how to make
rotis puff up on the stove
how to do her hair in twin buns
wear a chunni without pins
she taught me to drink rum coke,
stay out all night, cure a hangover

i licked the side of her face
told her she tastes like a rasgulla
she said i taste like cardamom and peaches
we laughed all the way into september

entanglements

she attends a christian private school
flirts a skirt with white girls
from eight to four
changes clothes at six into a salwar kameez
at seven we meet at gurdwara

our parents praying inside
outside she reveals how girls at school bind
her to the bike rack and heave dirt
on her. i clutch her hands tell her
i will marry her take her away
we play arranged marriage
we play bollywood dance
    my arranged husband
    i flutter my eyelashes
    she grasps my hand while
    the other travels to my lower back
    she hits her hips and shakes
    desire forward then back
    her turban unravels
    entangled in saris and smiles
    parents catch us
    drag us inside

inside the gurdwara
we rendezvous in the back left corner
mothers and fathers turn their heads
one-hundred degrees away
from god to check up on us
we spin plans to run away

my arranged husband doesn't show up for five days
she meets a white girl named andrea
who lets her colour jesus brown
on the sixth days she confesses
she kissed andrea on the lips

the other white girls called her pakiqueer

you are not allowed to kiss white girls
i punched her
mothers come rushing
blood all over the carpet
she is the first brown girl I punched

on the seventh day   i think she went to church to repent
or maybe we broke up

scene one: our first kiss

in an unfinished basement, we mimic bollywood
surmeet's sari pleated and tucked into her jeans
and draped over her shoulder the pallu long
enough to touch the floor, of course, she's dressed
in the latest fashion she plays sweet sweet shy
covers half her face

i, the man, with a homemade green turban
gaze at her lip-sync desires
a husband was what she needed,
i join in at the end
close-up scene his hand touches her face
she's not shy anymore
takes her hand and leads her to the piled-up blankets
guides her head to the pillow
a light touch of lips
lean in for a kiss we learn
that from hollywood
our first kiss

we plead for sleepovers
construct tent forts out
of heavy mink blankets
peek out and giggle at the world
flashes of a mother on the phone
brothers jumping over tents
fathers asleep in front of the tv
cover our heads fall asleep
dream of life together
#browngirllove

scene two: break-up

your engagement photo you are seated beside a man
you are dressed in last year's fashion, a drab salwar kameez
eyes fixed on mine a close up of terror
a perfected bollywood performance
in the movie when her father attempts to marry
her off to some older man
i swoop in on my broom-horse rescue her
always a happy ending kiss

but at your wedding
sandwiched between a mother-in-law and a not-me groom
as you get up the glare off your wedding jewellery blinds
we promised never to end this way
and the happily-ever-after-wedding-flash goes off
and here you sit my bollywood bride

hidden obedience

I.

diasporic hipster lived in shadows
my brother in the basement
i hid behind books
the other sisters loved hockey,
football, soccer anything to keep their eyes
glued to the television; we simply frowned
when dragged to the gurdwara
we sat cross-legged from six to nine sometimes eleven
without question

we waited out our parents
we tiptoed around after dark
drove home drunk
changed into jeans and tank tops in school bathrooms
once i left prayers to go to a poetry reading
only to return before the ardas

punjabis disperse across the city
there was no surveillance
to photograph our acts of rebellion
life was simple to be two people
have two lives one in Osborne Village
the other in St. Vital
effortless to slip
into another life

2.

had we screamed out loud
enjoyed the beatings, left home,
had a car crash, tore off our turbans,
chunnies, and kacheras,
brown-girl rebels that
got caught every time

you might still be alive
you might still be here
living a life
maybe an arranged marriage
maybe an off the grid contract
maybe a white life
but you would be a maybe
a searchable facebook life
we might be together

feminist instructions

dear married women
dear arranged married women
dear mothers
dear auntyji
dear masi
dear you

when he slaps you across the face:
when she slaps you across the face:
when they slap you across the face:

get a job and make sure the cheque is in your name.
open a bank account. i recommend a high interest saving account.
get a baseball bat. feel the weight. when no one is home, swing
break a lamp. listen to the crash. remember, you can make it happen.
if need be, repeat.

make a plan.
tell three people.
trust yourself.
never apologize.

love, love-marriage woman
love, arranged married woman
love, mothers
love, auntyji
love, masi
love, you

macro-love reaction

colour regulates who is allowed on the sidewalk
white kids will not allow you on the sidewalk

                              we find $10 on the road

colour controls who is allowed to board the airplane
colour adjusts who is allowed to be religious in public

            the airport security tells a man to take off his turban, he refuses.
            a stand-off. a hijab-wearing woman beside the sikh man explains:
            "he's sikh and the turban is sacred, how dare you ask such a thing"
                  he thanks his muslim sister as they walk to their gate

colour adjusts who is allowed to be religious in public
young white boys throw rocks at us when we leave our gurdwara

            the gurdwara's sangat allows the hindu's sangat to use their
            space while their temple is being built strength in numbers

colour normalizes who is allowed to decorate our lives
white women hang saris as curtains, charge $10 for scarfs

                        saris are handed down the generations
                  we decorate lineage with grandmother's teaching

colour polices who is allow to assist
cops do not know the difference between us

                              a black girl walks into the 7-11
                                    tells the turbaned man
                                    she's lost and hungry.
                              he. does. not. call. the. cops.
                                    he gives her a sandwich
                        calls his wife to walk the girl home.

pride march

- sat sir akala, taiaji
- oh, hello, patheeji
they stop in recognition

they saw his patheeji across the street:
they walked hand-in-hand
a south asian butch, with short black hair,
jeanshorts with glitter bare legs,
a rainbow muscle shirt, a little too tight
and her south asian femme girlfriend
in her form-fitting dress, low heels, make-up perfected
and holding up under the heat

they saw her taiaji across the street:
they walked hand-in-hand
a south asian bear in a flowing white linen shirt
with india's cricket team logo on the pocket,
bootyshorts a little too tight and his south asian boyfriend
in his pride flag sarong, pride beads bounced off his exposed
care-bear glitter belly

they walk in the middle of the road
took up space along the route
she with her girlfriend
he with his boyfriend

- just enjoying downtown?
- yes, just enjoy.
they left a little glitter rainbow trail behind them.

culinary camps

tali plates
chai tea
nanna bread
loonie toonies
canadians like double double words

daughters only inherit the recipes

a small stack of books under the coffee table
a daughter's unlearning
of rose petals candy arts degrees
a foundation of memory only the body holds DNA
the spit of rose fruit files
liquid release for our grandmothers
are no longer a performance of labour
is pink liquid fragility of inheritance

1984: junior master chef in training

i read romance horror novels
until mum's call.

10am first phone call:
pick out all the stones from the yellow lentils.
wash one cup, any cup is one cup,
the water runs clear.
let them soak.
dial tone _____.

1pm phone call number two:
drain and refill the pot with fresh water.
set to boil and watch it.
dial tone _____.

2pm phone call number three:
pinch a few lentils to check if they are cooked.
in another pot add oil,
add teaspoon of haldi, garam masala,
salt, chop up a tomato, hari mirch and onion
make the tardka and add to the lentils. do not burn the onions.
dial tone _____.

3pm phone call number four:
i'm coming home. start the roti.

bring me a slurpee. i like sprite.

dial tone _____.

1985: roti maps

first batch
thick   raw   full of lumps
thrown out.
dad, asked for rice.

second batch
overdone
hard   stiff   misshapened
brother refused to eat.
mum said to use the golden temple atta,
not the robinhood all-purpose flour,
all-purpose white was not to be trusted.
dad soaked his frisbee discs roti in daal
and served himself more daal.

creative with the third batch
roll large shapes of partition and whole india,
hudson bay, bootshape italy, ireland,
dad, i made kenya for you, he ate it,
and asked for england.

back to the basics for the fourth attempt
there is a reason why rotis
balloon   bellow up   round,
mum says when someone is hungry
roti will bubble up quick.
round   thin   soft
takes a full summer of daily practice
from noon to three.
dad, said he never ate so well.

1986: anatomy of knives

At the age of eleven,
my easy-bake kitchen:
contained
knifes, graters, stove, sandwich maker,
the usual steel pot full of canola oil for deep-frying
my summer toys

at home, we used steak knives
as vegetable peelers, as butter knives
the bluntness of blades
led me to believe that kirpans
were dull and could not cut anyone
knives, all sizes my weapon
when we marry, there will be no knives
we are not allowed to buy knives
as wedding presents or birthday gifts
a symbol of bad luck.

white-knuckled I held down a potato
knuckles red raw from slicing too closely
peeling onions skin towards myself
got me an *improper knife handling*
written on my home economic report card
deep frying: samosas, pakoras, puris,
cassava, and furfur was easy compared
to grade seven cooking class.

1986: instructions are on the side of the box

how are you going to feed your indian family, if you,
are going to toss food in the dumpster?

not boiling the water first
earned us a second sink of dishes,
in grade eight home economics.
we were told that we,
needed these skills.
if you dump the pasta in cold water,
the water will turn starch white
the macaroni sinks, fuses together,
bonds to the bottom of the pot.
Joni, my indian friend, looked at me, her indian friend,
we ate the pasta al dente with butter.

by eleven, Joni made grilled cheese sandwiches,
baked birthday cakes from scratch for her sisters,
impressed us all with chocolate ganache strawberries
as an after-school snack.
by ten years old, i was a phone call sous chef,
exceptional at trial and error cooking.
mum kept me inside the house
out of sun my sikh skin soaked up tanned browned crisp
what did Miss.HomeEc know?
#notfairandlovely #notreadyformarriage

kitchen gadgets

lock n' steam whistle
an alarm to run out of the kitchen
the science did not impress me
never use the pressure cooker
for channa, daal or kale chola;
trust me, you don't need the quickness

let chickpeas, lentils, black chickpeas
soak and boil on the stove
that's how you create your palate

i took the dubba of spice, tava, jaali, rolling pin,
and popcorn machine when i moved out

daily kitchen bombs
i knew how to recover:
lock n' steam whistle: run
tarka being made: hide in the basement
roti time: get the rolling pin and ghee

but love bombs set on simmer
my #pressurecookerlovelifeexplodes

instructions on managing the highs and lows

#eatsomething

#staywarm

yes, you.
a killjoy needs some time
in the sun to brown up,
tan naturally, soak up power
drink coconut, mango, lime, tamarind juices
as a killjoy, you will get all the benefits right away
powerup from the inside out.
when your winter coat feels like a body hug
it's time to book a ticket to the beach
lay in the sand watch body melt
stay until the sand and body
are the same temperature

#wpgsocials

your superpower is being invisible
people will buzz around you
as you stand in the middle of the room
pull all pieces together
learn how to survive in place
is the only option for us on the prairies
join the socials but try not to vomit in the snow

#eatingforone

eat cake for one meal, i suggest dinner,
have carrot cake, it's a good idea
to get a vegetable in there

clean your fridge every month
keep small bottles of champagne
when success happens, pop one open
drink from the bottle
no need for juice

#unplug

unplug everything
in your apartment
including the alarm clock

#satisfyingtheneedforslowspeed

go into London Drugs or the Bay
touch all the pressure cookers, slow cookers,
and crockpots with inserts
be serious about the whole affair
then ask the sales person for a regular pot with a lid.

#winnipegiscold

be a snowflake that yields a blizzard
you will not allow your feet to freeze
while walking over the Donald and Osborne bridges
cold toes are a body trigger.

#bealert

you will not walk with headphones on
you love music but it's not worth the
heartattack each time someone zooms past you
muffled sounds are a body trigger.

#tellingnotshowing

these are my instructions for us
to keep us alive.
remember divide courage
be open to the young brown faces
hold them and say, i see you
forgive them for forgetting
the daal on the stove

masis vs auntyji

aged out of youth
a cliché for white mainstream artists
but what of us, masis, as we like to call ourselves,
a small distinction but in the age of youth
tumbler to twitter to snapchat
masi stood here, walked here, fought battles here,
have been here before. masi left flowers in novels,
tears drops on paper, cut up their saris to include
pockets to carry artwork, notebooks, and pencils.
masi did not provide you with survival skills rather
artful degrees and gallery spaces

masi only understood the weight of boundaries
a hula hoop of breakage
brown skin not a protective shield
a degree or two, a double pane window,
kept heat in our gaze out
that is what masi learned early on

masi tears up at photos unable to capture
an inward fresh-off-the-boat stereotypes
of young brown queers,
body hair kept against mehndi tattoos
gold chains, body gardens
a torso of a wedding dress
here the inward
outworld of digital photos

masi thread twist your upper lip
twist uproot body tiny hairs
visible under a magnifying mirror
or only to your lover
#threadinglife

instructions on how to love yourself

demand a hairstyle and stylist
break all the religious rules once, then again, trust this poem.
finger your girlfriend; remember clip your fingernails.
pierce and tattoo every body part. make yourself beautiful.
rent an apartment be as messy as you want.
orgasms are real and yes, you can have one or six in an escapade.

bollywood cowgirl
#backatyourplace

my madhuri dixit

watch bollywood clips on the indian channel
brown women sway hips and shake fingers
dress in their indian power-suit;
tight crop tops with floor length lenghas
bright rouge lips   see-though chunnis
women linger control over brown men
familiar dance into lusty affairs

you twirl around the kitchen with wooden spoon microphone
your athletic frame able-bodied dance
persuade me to sashay towards you
circle your head with ten-dollar bills
throw money at your feet
kitchen dance lip-sync battles
we fulfill our teenage selves
that never left the house
fear of cultural reprimand
from auntyjis and white friends

you invoked a bollywood aesthetic
before it was cool
with your burgundy bedroom walls
indian inspired rosewood cabinets
footstools, bolsters, that you bought at the local market
we think ourselves indian with a lowercase i
we swoon together create new steps
dressed in jeans, t-shirts that are made in india
never did we think that we were bollywood royalty
in the middle of the prairies

my aishwarya rai

we watch *Devdas*,
on saturday night
i tap on your thigh,
i play tap on your thigh
i play tabla on your thigh
i play tabla on your thigh
sunday morning.

we watched *Devdas* again,
a patriarchal film, cheesy bollywood
lines mimic the swagger
you dress in sari
only to be unwrapped

reading tabla poetry

i learn tabla poems
on your thigh
you tell me my hands strike soft
heaviness felt on your heart

these are new love poems
only to be written again

sunday night watching

i always wanted to play the tabla   practice on me
play the tabla on our escapade
thigh, hipbone, up your curve and over to earlobe
top of your head back down
earlobe to over and curve your up, hipbone, thigh
practice on me
i always wanted to play the tabla

#lovebombsiloveyou

we take cover under sheets
lighting sparks each wave
your lips find my neck
a flash before a kiss
airtight locked lips
we are living inside a pressure cooker,
you said kisses heat lips steam
increase temperature to perfection

unlock the lid
i always thought the house was going to explode,
the pressure cooker on high whistle
you laugh at the thought of lentil shrapnel
it's not a bomb until we add explosives that will
trigger an electrical charge
we add a nose ring, a belly button piercing,
we spark change
static ignites sheets ripple heartbeat

macaroni love affair

the day you came out of surgery
informing me you were itchy
all over from morphine
i held your hands
joked about scratching
your heart out

you told me you waited for nurses
to bring you macaroni dinner
that was a signal that you
could go home
i made you macaroni dinner
every day after that waiting for you to eat
boxes of kd in my kitchen

i told you water stories, so you could pee
there was a lake it gushed blue water
you thought i was a poet but i didn't have good stories
i was just trying to get us out of rockyview

it worked and we went home

golden repair fail

the day you told me you felt broken
i tried to hold you together like a samosa
a playful try, i held your face instead
called you my potato filling

your body broke more that summer
like the ancient art of *kintsugi,*
golden repair of ceramics
you laughed at the thought of me
as a golden fixer and you as pot
the day you said i don't remember any of these conversations
of course, i said, you were high on morphine
all i could do was watch
feed you pasta noodles one by one
from a broken bowl

there will be another visit to rockyview

rom-com

the day you were back in the hospital
i walked all the way to the operating room
beside your bed, we joked about Junior Mints

i didn't know about the swinging door
Authorized Personal and Patients Only Sign:
straight out of a romantic comedy
you laughed when i stood
on my tiptoes to peek in at you.
we will play this game five years later
in another city, different circumstance
i wait for you to come home from work, peek out the front window,
a love habit, you are my second day, two days rolled into one.

i waited for you all day
walked the grounds
stared at smokers outside
tried to find a chapel
but only found the cafeteria

rom-com sequel

love followed me around the hospital
love made sure i did not trip on my walk
love made sure i did not start smoking
love made sure i did not find the chapel
because love knew it would be a bad scene, me, in a chapel
love found me a sandwich, tea, and biscuits
love knew i had a tupperware of mac n'cheese,
and knew it was not going to be eaten today
or tomorrow love knew i would keep making it everyday
love knew i hated hospitals but love knew i would not leave
until i could squeeze your hand
love knew I ate all the Junior Mints

love knows how love set on low marinates and cures

sweet like jalebi

Someone said this is your first lover, you will never want to leave her.
Dionne Brand

i let the words fly
like a lover tossing her lover
a rope to climb *kiss me for real*
you kissed me
that day i had my eyes closed
body navigates
knows love
like it knows heat
over skin sunlight bright
to open eyes

body melts takes a shape it remembers
breathes life back into forgotten moments
opens your mouth a taste of syrup set me ablaze

side of your neck, i lick,
suck on your earlobe
you are sweet like jalebi
you smell of the candy aisle
sticky on my lips a lick up and in around
i suck sweet out you will be my first lover
you will linger take me into your mouth

i tell you that i want to grow old
with you when i'm old i'll garden
in overalls and rainbow rain boots
no bra no underwear
every evening we will have jalebis
in hot milk

it will be years later before,
i write a different poem for you
these poems will spoon you like a poem should
but for right now *kiss me for real again and again
and just for you, again*

mid-language semi complete

it will be years later when
i will be able to write a different poem for you
i will step closer write body scars
against cheek forehead into belly
these poems will be in a new language full

these words written at the beginning
this poem is written at the ten-year mark
one hundred- and twenty-months to show
how to fill in the whole piece

mid-life escapade

fill in gaps with hearts
find stone shaped hearts on sidewalks
painted balloon shaped hearts on building sides
graffiti hearts, reality shaped nonsense hearts
we need to pick up hearts
we need to teach young ones to cut out
hearts out of construction paper red,
brown, orange, yellow, green, blue, purple, black
instead kiss hearts suck sweet out of each of us
wake up heart-shaped hold hands
we need love poems now
#lovemenow

selected glossary

ardas	prayer
atta	flour
auntyji	all-purpose term for related or unrelated women
chacha	father's brother
chachi	wife of father's brother
chana / chole	chickpeas
chimta	tongs
chuni	long material used to cover one's head
daal	lentil soup
dadiji	paternal grandmother
furfur	puffed up rice chips
gori	white woman
gurdwara	sikh temple
guru	teacher or spiritual guide
guru granth sahib	religious text of the sikh faith
gulab jamum	sweets made from milk and soaked in rose sugar syrup
haldi	turmeric
izzat	honour
jaali	mesh grill
jalebi	deepfried sweetness!
juda	hair tied up and coved with cloth
kachera	underpants
kameez	a shirt-like top
kara	a steel bracelet
kesh	hair, unshorn hair
kirpan	a curved knife
langar	sikh dining hall
masi	mother's sister
michi	chili
mithai	sweets made from milk or wheat

nanak	religious founder of the sikh faith
patheeji	niece
rasgulla	sweetmilk round cakes
roti(s)	an unleavened flatbread
salwar	baggy trousers
seva	service to god
tabla	drums
taiaji	father's older brother
tardka	usually a browning of onions, ginger and garlic
tava	flat pan to make roti
thali	platter with divided sections

acknowledgements

To my poetry muse: Sharron Proulx-Turner, thank you for placing hearts in my path. I see them everywhere; in branches, pebbles, snow drifts, and on sign posts.

Thank you to Micheline Maylor for believing in this manuscript. Thank you to Neil Petrunia for the design.

Thank you to Divya Mehra and Sheniz Janmohamed for all our creative conversations over chai, coffee, and wine!

Two poems featured here have appeared in one form or another: *masis vs auntyji* and *daughters only inherit the recipes* were written as creative responses for an art exhibition in Gallery 1C03. Thank you to Noor Bhangu, the curator for *Not the Camera, But the Filing Cabinet* for displaying work by emerging artists. Thank you to Ayqa Khan and Christina Hajjar for your creative work.

Thank you to Hannah Green, Ashley Au, Chimwemwe Undi, and all the creative minds at *Contemporary Verse 2: The Canadian Journal of Poetry and Critical Writing (CV2)*. Thank you to Clarise Foster, for reading earlier version of this manuscript. Thank you to the QT/BIPOC writing community in Winnipeg, thank you for inviting me to read parts of this book at *Drop the Mic.*

references

The following poetry books were companions during
the writing of this book:

Brand, Dionne. *No Language Is Neutral.*
Coach House Press, 1990.

Janmohamed, Sheniz. *Firesmoke : Poems.*
TSAR Publications, 2014.

MacFayden, Laurie. *Kissing Keeps Us Afloat.*
Frontenac House Poetry, 2014.

Pal, Rajinderpal S. *Pulse : Poems.*
Arsenal Pulp Press, 2002.

Proulx-Turner, Sharron. *The Trees Are Still Bending South.*
Kegedonce Press, 2012.

biography

Sharanpal Ruprai is an Assistant Professor in the Department of Women's and Gender Studies at the University of Winnipeg. Sharanpal Ruprai's début poetry collection, *Seva*, was chosen as a finalist for the Stephan G. Stephansson Award for Poetry by the Alberta Literary Awards. Her poetry is featured in a number of anthologies: *GUSH: Menstrual Manifestos for Our Time*, *The Calgary Renaissance*, *Red Silk: An Anthology of South Asian Canadian Women Poets*, and *Exposed*. *Pressure Cooker Love Bomb* is her second collection of poetry.